T0011947

THE LITTLE GUIDE TO

BRUCE SPRINGSTEEN

This edition published in 2023 by OH!
An Imprint of Welbeck Non-Fiction Limited,
part of Welbeck Publishing Group.
Offices in: London – 20 Mortimer Street, London W1T 3JW
and Sydney – Level 17, 207 Kent St, Sydney NSW 2000 Australia
www.welbeckpublishing.com

ISBN 978-1-80069-529-0

Compiled and written by: Malcolm Croft
Editorial: Victoria Denne
Project manager: Russell Porter
Design: Tony Seddon
Production: Jess Brisley

A CIP catalogue record for this book is available from the British Library

Printed in China

10 9 8 7 6 5 4 3 2 1

THE LITTLE GUIDE TO
BRUCE SPRINGSTEEN

THE BOSS

CONTENTS

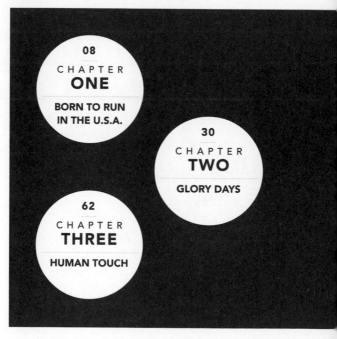

INTRODUCTION

Bruce Springsteen is *the* world's greatest boss. As the leader of the E Street Band, the singer's life-long motley crew of beloved New Jersey noiseniks, he's in charge, giving them something to sing about for more than 50 years. But Bruce is more than the boss of the band; he's the boss of America's soul, too, musically and spiritually. And he has been since 1973 when the 22-year-old singer-songwriter hit the stages of his hometown's dive bars with two incredible albums already popping out from under his blue-collar belt.

From even his earliest (and now infamous) shows, Bruce was canonized as the Patron Saint of the Working Man, earning that title for songs which were inspired by—and a celebration of—working-class Americans, just like his father, Doug. And while Bruce's father "never really cared" for his son's songs (a source of bitter and brave inspiration for a young Bruce), the rest of the U.S.

and then the whole world couldn't wait to be all ears. And it hasn't stopped listening ever since.

In his generation-spanning career on the run in the U.S.A., Bruce has received critical and commercial adoration for crafting lyrics and music that symbolized the everyday stories of his, and his home nations history; songs that often spat with passion and purpose, stinging political vitriol and, the sweetest of soul-spangled melodies. No other singer-songwriter has captured, or championed, America's heart and soul more than Bruce. Not yet at least.

This little book of the world's No.1 Boss is a brilliant bundle of wit and wisdom taken straight from the musician's mighty mouth, a tiny tome that celebrates his wonderful way with words, his lyrical poetry and life philosophies, and defining precisely what it means to be born in the U.S.A.... and beyond!

CHAPTER
ONE

BORN TO RUN IN THE U.S.A.

Bruce's biggest song and album—"Born to Run" and *Born in the USA*—were borne out of the singer's desire to better understand his broken nation, his hometown of New Jersey and his family (i.e. his dad, Doug), as well as escape from his past. But no matter how far he traveled, he could never outrun his roots.

Let's join our Bruce now on the long and winding road of his running career. We guarantee it's going to be the ride of a lifetime…

I always knew what I wanted to do and where I was going. Anything other than music was always a dead-end for me.

Bruce, on his ambitions, interview with Jeff Burger, *Zoo World*, March 14, 1974.

I ain't makin' that much money.
I've got some great musicians
in my band and I'm payin' them
terrible money. I pay myself the
same, but it's terrible for me,
too. I mean, we're barely makin'
a livin', barely scrapin' by.

"

Bruce, on his earliest moneymaking performing live,
interview with Jeff Burger, *Zoo World*, March 14, 1974.

❝

It was definitely 'make or break' at the time. I knew it was what I wanted to create, but I didn't know if it was going to save me from being tossed off a record company at the time. At the time, I was held in very low esteem at my record company.

❞

Bruce, on his career after his false-start debut albums in 1973, interview with BBC News, 2016.

When I was a boy there were two things in my house that my parents didn't like. One was me. The other was the guitar. 'That goddam guitar!' my father used to say. I think he thought all the things in my room were made by the same company, 'That Goddamn guitar! The Goddamn stereo! Those Goddamn records!'

Bruce, on that goddamn guitar, interview with Robert Duncan, *Creem Magazine*, October 1978.

Bruce was raised Catholic and attended the nun-run St Rose of Lima High School, in Freehold, New Jersey. However, he hated it. "In the third grade, a nun stuffed me in a garbage can under her desk because she said that's where I belonged!" Bruce told *Rolling Stone*.

The future singer often rebelled against the religious scripture and strictures imposed upon him, preferring instead to stay in his bedroom and learn "Twist and Shout" on the guitar.

One day my parents called me downstairs for a talk. And they sit me down at the kitchen table with them and they start telling me it's about time I start getting serious with my life. 'And don't tell me about that goddamn guitar!' my father said.

Bruce, on his parents, interview with Robert Duncan, *Creem Magazine*, October 1978.

"

We came up in a golden age for what we did. If you were a young guy playing a guitar in 1967, 1975, or 1985 you came up just as that whole business turned into something that no one ever thought it would, and we were like the ball players—that got paid. You know, instead of the guys like Mickey Mantle, who were incredible— that was before they paid you.

"

Bruce, on the '70s music industry, interview with Howard Stern, *The Howard Stern Show*, November 27, 2022.

Probably done something crazy. Maybe robbed stores! That always appealed to me, robbing things.

Bruce, when asked what he would be if not a musician, interview with Ray Coleman, *Melody Maker*, 1975.

I was pretty much a misfit in my own town. Me and a few other guys were the town freaks and there were many occasions when we were dodging getting beaten up ourselves.

Bruce, on his teenage years in New Jersey, interview with Judy Wieder, *The Advocate*, 1996.

I was a serious young man. I had serious ideas about rock music. I believed that serious things could be done with it. It had a power; it had a voice. I still fucking believe that.

Bruce, on the power of rock music, interview with Judy Wieder, *The Advocate*, 1996.

One night I was standing between George Harrison and Mick Jagger. As a boy, I sat in my room with their records, I learned to play my guitar from those records. I studied every riff and the way they played it, and my initial bands were modeled on them. I was like 'Hey, what am I doing here?'

Bruce, on meeting his heroes, interview with Gavin Martin, *NME*, March 9, 1996.

I kept my promises. I didn't get burned out. I didn't waste myself. I didn't die. I didn't throw away my musical values. I've dug in my heels on all those things. And my music has been, for the most part, a positive, liberating, living, uplifting thing. And along the way I've made a lot of money, and I bought a big house.

Bruce, on his career promises, interview with James Henke, *Rolling Stone*, August 6, 1992.

"

I still love New Jersey.
We go back all the time.
But I came out to L.A.,
and I just felt like the guy
who was born in the U.S.A.
had left the bandanna
behind, you know?

"

Bruce, on leaving his past where it belongs, interview
with James Henke, *Rolling Stone*, August 6, 1992.

I never felt at home even when I was home.

Bruce, on his difficult childhood, interview with
Mike Parker, *The Express*, May 22, 2011.

66

My parents moved away to California when I was 19. I stayed in New Jersey, so none of us [in the E Street Band] was really connected to our folks, and so we all sort of bonded together and we created our own family.

99

Bruce, on the E Street Band, radio interview with RAI, May 1993.

Bruce has been the frontman of his beloved E Street Band for more than forty years, with some time off for good behavior!

However, before this iconic band got together in the mid-'70s, Bruce founded several other bands, including the Rogues, Southside Johnny and the Asbury Jukes, the Castiles, Earth, and Steel Mill.

When I walk out on stage there is a moment of tremendous identity confirmation, it's a moment when I'm finding out about who I am, who's my audience, and what are we saying to each other. All those things coming to play when you go on stage, and I think it just keeps me burning long through the night.

Bruce, on performing live, radio interview with RAI, May 1993.

"

I put together a real Hendrix/
Cream three-piece group called
Earth for quite a while.
That was the 'Day of the
Guitarist'—Alvin Lee and Jeff
Beck and Clapton and Hendrix.
And locally I was the guitarist—
the fast gun at the time.

"

Bruce, on playing lead guitar in his earliest band,
interview with Bill Flanagan, *Musician*, November 1992.

66

I was typecast as an acoustic act for a while. Locally I took a tremendous amount of heat when the first record came out; I had such a big local reputation in the Jersey area as a hard-rockin' guitar band that when the first record came out people were sort of, 'What happened?'

99

Bruce, on his 1973 debut album *Greetings From Asbury Park, New Jersey*, interview with Bill Flanagan, *Musician*, November 1992.

> **"**
>
> I didn't sing in the Castiles, my first band. I basically played the guitar. Everybody in the band felt that I couldn't sing at all.
>
> **"**

Bruce, on his first band, interview with Bill Flanagan, *Musician*, November 1992.

CHAPTER
TWO

GLORY DAYS

Bruce used his songs as a stepping stone (the origin of his surname in Dutch—a Springsteen, FYI) to break away from his past. Thankfully, though, he took the whole of E Street along for the ride with him.

As fame and fortune came knocking, Bruce was ready to knock 'em down dead. Welcome to the rise (and fall) of Bruce's glory days…

You make your record like it's the last record you'll ever make. There's no tomorrows and there's no yesterdays. There's only right now.

Bruce, on making records, interview with
Dave DiMartino, *Creem Magazine*, January 1981.

66

There's a thin line between mental illness and creativity. I don't know many artists who are not crazy. I think that's why you get into it. You're in pursuit of a certain sort of peace that's very, very, very difficult to come by.

99

Bruce, on mental illness and creativity, interview with Jeffrey Brown, *PBS*, December 20, 2016.

I'd been listening to Duane Eddy, the twangy guitar sound, Roy Orbison, the very unusually and unstructured songs, and Bob Dylan. Those are the three things that kind of found their way into *Born to Run* because I was never really much of a revolutionary musician…but I was an alchemist. I put a lot of things together along with stuff I pulled up out of myself.

Bruce, on his early influences for *Born to Run*, interview with BBC News, 2016.

"

After *Born to Run*, I had a reaction to my good fortune. With success, it felt like a lot of people who'd come before me lost some essential part of themselves. My greatest fear was that success was going to change or diminish that part of myself.

"

Bruce, on his early fame and success, interview with Keith Cameron, *The Guardian*, September 23, 2010.

'Born to Run', that expands every time we go out on tour. It's always a huge catharsis. It's fascinating to see the audience singing it back to me. It's quite wonderful to see people that intensely singing your song.

Bruce, on performing "Born to Run" live for 40 years, interview with Terry Gross, *NPR*, October 5, 2016.

Somewhere between
realization and actualization,
I slipped in between
the cracks.

Bruce, on his mental health, interview with
James Henke, *Rolling Stone*, August 6, 1992.

I came from a small town. The subversiveness of the top 40 radio can't be over-estimated. I grew up on music that was popular. I sat in my bedroom, and I wrote the top 40 down religiously every Wednesday night, cheering for my heroes and hissing the villains of the day.

"

Bruce, on his first connections to pop music in the 1960s, interview with Neil Strauss, *Guitar World*, October 1995.

The town I grew up in was very divided, racially and class-wise; and yet there were songs that united everyone at some point, like the great Motown music.

Bruce, on music as a unifier, interview with Neil Strauss, *Guitar World*, October 1995.

Ever wondered how Springsteen got his famous nickname—"The Boss"?

Funny story. Springsteen was known as The Boss for years before he made it famous. In the early 1970s, when Springsteen and the E Street Band played gigs in tiny venues such as Stone Pony and Max's Castle, it was Bruce's job (as frontman) to collect gig earnings and pay the rest of the band. This led them to start calling him "The Boss", a nickname that stuck.

Springsteen—a fierce believer of workers' rights—naturally dislikes this nickname! "I hate bosses. I hate being called the boss," he once said.

I've had a long life with my audience. Every now or then a guy will yell at me through his car window. 'Hey, Bruce, we need you!' or I get a few letters that read, 'Hey, man, we need you.' Or I bump into some people at a club, and they say, 'Hey, we need you.' They don't really need me, but I'm proud if they need what I do. That's what my band is. That's what we were built for.

Bruce, on fan appreciation, interview with Jann Wenner, *Rolling Stone*, September 22, 2004.

"

There were two kinds of kids
when I first started out. There
were the kinds of kids who
threw themselves into the
'60s, and there were guys
who continued to lead a life
of the '50s. I went one way.
My sister went the other and
lived a very working-class,
blue-collar, New Jersey life.

"

Bruce, on the changing culture of the 1960s, interview
with Joe Heim, *Washington Post*, April 12, 2009.

> 66
>
> I'm a lifetime musician; I'm going to be playing music forever. I don't foresee a time when I would not be onstage somewhere, playing a guitar and playing it loud, with power and passion. I look forward to being sixty-five and doing just that!
>
> 99

Bruce, on staying relevant in the music industry, interview with James Henke, *Rolling Stone*, August 6, 1992.

66

At the end of the *Born in the U.S.A.* tour and after we made the live album, I felt like it was the end of the first part of my journey. And then, for the *Tunnel of Love* tour, I switched where people had stood for fifteen years, just trying to give it a different twist. I wanted to get rid of some of the old expectations.

99

Bruce, on defying audience expectations, interview with James Henke, *Rolling Stone*, August 6, 1992.

I really enjoyed the success of *Born in the U.S.A.*, but by the end of that whole thing, I just kind of felt 'Bruced' out. I was like 'Whoa, enough of that.' You end up creating this sort of icon, and eventually it oppresses you.

Bruce, on *Born in the U.S.A.*, interview with James Henke, *Rolling Stone*, August 6, 1992.

Bruce named his primary touring band the E Street Band after the address 1105 E Street, Belmar, New Jersey, where keyboardist David Sanctious' mother lived. She allowed the band to rehearse in her garage.

One day, Springsteen saw a street sign, and started saying it over and over: "E Street, E Street. E Street Band. Yeah."

The whole image that had been created—and that I'm sure I promoted—it always felt like 'Hey, that's not me.' The macho thing, that was just never me. It might be a little more of me than I think, but when I was a kid, I was a real gentle child.

Bruce, on his alpha-male stage persona of the 1980s, interview with James Henke, *Rolling Stone*, August 6, 1992.

"

There's so many things I could do that I haven't done yet, so many ways of presenting the music that I haven't done that I'm anxious to do. In the '90s I want to do a lot of different things.

"

Bruce, on career reinvention in the 1990s, interview with Bill Flanagan, *Musician*, November 1992.

"

I thought *Born in the U.S.A.* would be a popular record; I didn't think it would be the thing it ended up being. That's just what happened. I thought *Tunnel of Love* would be more popular, but that's what happened there. Hey, you ride along with it.

"

Bruce, on his rising and falling popularity, interview with Bill Flanagan, *Musician*, November 1992.

Some of the best things I learned were learned from getting beat up, making mistakes. And if you're afraid to do that, to step out and fall, that's living in fear. If you can't take the pain you're not going to get to that higher place.

Bruce, on making mistakes, interview with Bill Flanagan, *Musician*, November 1992.

All my music is a journey towards some sort of connection with both people at large and then a person, whether it's in your family or your girlfriend or your wife. That's how you remain vital and don't get lost in the furniture that comes with making a few bucks.

Bruce, on making connections with his audience, interview with David Hepworth, *Q Magazine*, August 1992.

When President Barack Obama presented Bruce with the prestigious Kennedy Center Award in 2009—the highest honor awarded to U.S. civilians—Obama introduced Bruce, saying: "I'm the President...but Bruce is the boss."

For me, my music is about trying to take down the walls that I had left up.

Bruce, on the purpose of his songs, interview with David Hepworth, *Q Magazine*, August 1992.

"

You do your best work, and you hope that it pulls out the best in your audience and some piece of it spills over into the real world and into people's everyday lives, and it takes the edge off of fear and allows us to recognize each other through our veil of differences.

"

Bruce, on the impact of his art, Academy Award Acceptance Speech for "Streets of Philadelphia", 1993.

I was lucky I survived the motorcycle accident because the bike went under the car. I flew out about 20 or 25 feet, I didn't have a helmet on, I hit my head on the pavement and knocked myself out, gave myself a brain concussion, screwed up my left leg. I was lucky then that I didn't get killed but I took a pretty good beating.

Bruce, on a near-fatal motorcycle collision with a '63 Cadillac in 1967, interview with Terry Gross, *NPR*, October 5, 2016.

I come out on stage to deliver to you the greatest band in the world. I still have great pride in what I do. I still believe in its power. I believe in my ability to transfer its power to you. One of the things our band was very good at communicating was that sense of joy, which I think makes us somewhat unique. Rock bands try to project a lot of different things: intensity, mystery, sexuality, cool. Not a lot of rock bands concentrate on joy.

Bruce, on live music as joy, interview with
Michael Hann, *The Guardian*, October 30, 2016.

Success makes life easier. It doesn't make LIVING easier.

Bruce, on success, interview with David Hepworth, *Q Magazine*, August 1992.

I came out of a working-class environment, played in working-class bars, and my history just drew me towards those topics naturally. I didn't have any particular political world view or any rhetoric which I was trying to get across in any way. It was just those were the things that felt urgent. I wrote a lot about that and I'm proud of that music. But I felt at the end of *Born in the U.S.A.* that I'd said all I wanted to say about those things. My battles were then elsewhere.

99

Bruce, on his hometown as songwriting inspiration, interview with David Hepworth, *Q Magazine*, August 1992.

66

I don't write for one side of the street. But the Bush years were so horrific you could not just sit around. It was such a blatant disaster. I campaigned for John Kerry and Barack Obama, and I am glad I did. But normally I would prefer to stay on the sidelines. The artist is supposed to be the canary in the cage.

99

Bruce, on his political position, interview with Fiachra Gibbons, *The Guardian*, February 17, 2012.

Patti [Scialfa] joined the
E Street Band back in 1985 and
around that time, I discovered
things in life that no school
had ever taught me to cope
with. I had never learned how
you get on with women!

Bruce, on his wife, and bandmember, interview with
Mans Ivarsson, *Beats Magazine*, August 1992.

In my job, you can get so locked into a particular image the people have of you. After you've been playing for 15 years, everybody has a very specific 'you' that they want you to be.

Bruce, on breaking expectations, interview with MTV Europe, March 1993.

CHAPTER
THREE

HUMAN TOUCH

The original working-class hero, Bruce has that everyman essence and charm that made him appeal to the red, white and blue-collar workers of America's tired, poor, and huddled masses.

He became an icon of a nation rapidly becoming disillusioned by the broken American Dream. He had the human touch capable of connecting with fans on an almost spiritual level.

With his prolific output, Bruce gave his countrymen something new to believe in: each other. Here's why...

> **"**
>
> When you embark on a creative life, you are partially directing it, and you are partially riding the wave. If your work is threaded into people's lives and into the life of your town, your family, your country, then you're like everybody else—you're at the mercy of events, you're borne along on the currents of time and history.
>
> **"**

Bruce, on the creative life, interview with Jann Wenner, *Rolling Stone*, September 22, 2004.

Bruce has never had
a number-one single in
America or the UK.

The singer Manfred Mann,
however, did take
Bruce's song, "Blinded by
the Light" to the top of
the charts in 1976.

After my first album came out, I remember [Bruce's early manager] Mike Appel called me and I said, 'How did we do?' He said, 'We didn't do very well, we sold about 20,000 records.' I said, '20,000 records! That's fabulous! I don't know 20,000 people. Who would buy a record by someone they have no idea about?'

Bruce, on his underwhelming sales to his 1972 debut album, interview with Adam Sweeting, *Uncut Magazine*, September 2002.

Why did I only feel good on the road? Why were all my characters in my songs in cars? In my early twenties, I was always sort of like 'Hey, what I can put in this suitcase, that guitar case, that bus—that's all I need, now and forever.' I didn't want to be one of those guys who can write music and tell stories and have an effect on people's lives, and maybe on society in some fashion, but not be able to get to know his own self.

Bruce, on running as a lyrical leitmotif, interview with James Henke, *Rolling Stone*, August 6, 1992.

I've always believed that people don't really listen to my music to find out about me, they listen to my music to find out about themselves.

Bruce, on fans, radio interview with WUNAW-FM, August 7, 1992.

In the past I think one of the
reasons I went on the road
was to escape—to search
for adventure or experience.

Bruce, on life touring the road, interview with
Bill Flanagan, *Musician*, November 1992.

I'd like to thank my mother, Adele, for that slushy Christmas Eve, when we stood outside the music store and I pointed to that Sunburst guitar and she had $60 bucks and I said, 'I need that one, Ma.' She got me what I needed, and she protected me and provided for me on a thousand other days and nights.

Bruce, on his mother, Induction into the Rock 'n Roll Hall of Fame speech, 1999.

66

What would I conceivably have written about without him? I mean, you can imagine that if everything had gone great between us, we would have had disaster. I would have written just happy songs. And I tried it in the early '90s and it didn't work; the public didn't like it.

99

Bruce, on his father as his muse (and his '90s career), Induction into the Rock 'n Roll Hall of Fame speech, 1999.

I was never a visionary like Bob Dylan, I wasn't a revolutionary, but I had the idea of a long arc: where you could take the job that I did and create this long emotional arc that found its own kind of richness. Thirty-five years staying connected to that idea. That's why I think the band continues to improve. You can't be afraid of getting old. Old is good, if you're gathering in life.

99

Bruce, on growing old with his band and career longevity, interview with Keith Cameron, *The Guardian*, September 23, 2010.

The first song Bruce learned to play on the guitar was the Beatles' "Twist and Shout". The song remains a live favorite, often as an encore.

Bruce and Paul McCartney performed it together at Bruce's London Hyde Park concert in 2012. It was a particular highlight for Bruce.

> **"**
> The wonderful thing about my job is that you can revisit your 22-year-old self or your 24-year-old self any particular night you want.
> **"**

Bruce, on choosing earlier songs for tour setlists, interview with Terry Gross, *NPR*, October 5, 2016.

BRUCE SPRINGSTEEN

It's funny, when we first came out, everyone tagged us as being a New York band, which we never really were. We were from Jersey, which was very different. New York was a million miles away. You didn't talk about it; you didn't think about it. It was all very local. That's the way those little towns and stuff are—you just never get out.

99

Bruce, on New Jersey, interview with Dave DiMartino, *Creem Magazine*, January 1981.

The way I look at it is I get paid to write a new song. I can't keep rewriting the old stuff.

Bruce, on pushing creative boundaries, interview with David Hepworth, *Q Magazine*, August 1992.

People tend to believe that everything an artist sings is self-experienced, but in reality that's only a part of what you're singing. But I guess my whole work is an emotional diary. The guy in 'Living Proof' is the same guy as the one in 'Born to Run', except he's covered a lot of miles in between.

Bruce, on singing about himself through his song's characters, interview with Mans Ivarsson, *Beats Magazine*, August 1992.

I know that an audience is hard to find. And it's easy to take that audience for granted. I think that if you subvert what you're saying, what you're doing, what you want your work or your life to be about, then you've lost yourself and the essence of what you do.

Bruce, on his audience and fans, interview with Bob Costas, "Columbia Records Radio Hour", November 21, 1995.

I felt I lived the prototypical American life—the way I grew up, the town I grew up in, my family life. Things that I cared about, things that I aspired to, they were just something that naturally came to me when I wrote. It cannot be abandoned and is worth fighting and fighting and fighting for.

Bruce, on fighting for the American way of life, interview with Jann Wenner, *Rolling Stone*, September 22, 2004.

Bruce's first ever
show as a signed artist was
as the opening act for
Dave van Ronk, at a gig at
Max's Kansas City venue in
New York in 1972.

He was just 23 years old.
He performed "Growin'
Up" and "Henry Boy".

66

I love my job and I love the things that it's brought me. If I had a choice, I'd do without that fame, but it comes with the territory. What's important is what's happening, not what's written about what's happening. Who cares? It's just not real. The reality of your own life overwhelms whatever bullshit somebody's written about you in a newspaper for a couple of days. It's not really your life.

99

Bruce, on fame and critics, interview with David Hepworth, *Q Magazine*, August 1992.

Yes, I make a setlist. I send it out to the band. We will do it on the first day of rehearsal. But it'll change by the second day.

Bruce, on making setlists for each new tour, interview with Andy Greene, *Rolling Stone*, November 18, 2022.

"

What I do is a very simple thing. I tell my team, 'Go out and see what everybody else is doing. Let's charge a little less.' That's generally the directions. They go out and set it up. For the past 49 years or however long we've been playing, we've pretty much been out there under market value. I've enjoyed that. It's been great for the fans.

"

Bruce, on under-charging his fans for tour ticket prices, interview with Andy Greene, *Rolling Stone*, November 18, 2022.

I didn't have a blueprint from my childhood that I could call on, which is an enormous deficit when you're trying to put together a family life. I didn't see a family life where men were thriving inside of it. My dad tended to blame the family for his inability to achieve what he wanted to achieve.

Bruce, on his father and becoming a father, interview with Terry Gross, *NPR*, October 5, 2016.

> **"**
>
> I think I was a little unusual in that I went into rock 'n' roll music to create order out of my life. My younger life felt rather chaotic, so I was in search of some stability, actually, some order.
>
> **"**

Bruce, on becoming a musician, interview with Michael Hann, *The Guardian*, October 30, 2016.

I walk on stage, I play,
I perform. And that's
sort of where that peace
comes over me.

Bruce, on the power of performing live, interview
with Jeffrey Brown, *PBS*, December 20, 2016.

In my business you're afforded the luxury of extended adolescence.

Bruce, on showbusiness, interview with
David Hepworth, *Q Magazine*, August 1992.

I have spent my life judging the distance between American reality and the American dream.

Bruce, on the American Dream, interview with Fiachra Gibbons, *The Guardian*, February 17, 2012.

I've had an enormous amount of luck and fortune and have worked hard, but that other thing—failure—never feels that far away.

Bruce, on failure, interview with Bob Costas, "Columbia Records Radio Hour", November 21, 1995.

66

I love my music, but I didn't want to try to distort it into being my entire life. Because that's a lie. It's not true. It's not your entire life. It never can be.

99

Bruce, on life outside of music, interview with James Henke, *Rolling Stone*, August 6, 1992.

I always saw myself as
the kid who stepped
up out of the front row
and onto the stage.

Bruce, on his connection with his audience, interview
with Neil Strauss, *Guitar World*, October 1995.

There is nothing more personal than the music people listen to. I know from my own experience how you identify and relate to the person singing. You have put your fingerprints on their imagination. That is very, very intimate. When something cracks the mirror, it can be hard for the fan who you have asked to identify with you.

Bruce, on fans identifying with artists, interview with Jann Wenner, *Rolling Stone*, September 22, 2004.

I know what it takes to write a song, and it's hard and you don't write that many and you pour your blood and sweat into it.

Bruce, on songwriting, interview with Adam Sweeting, *Uncut Magazine*, September 2002.

When you're locked into a period of creativity it's very similar to being hungry all the time. Everywhere you go you're hungry. So I might come up with a verse sitting at the kitchen table, I might be asleep and wake up in the middle of the night and run upstairs to my writing room and come up with another verse or two. Literally, I do it anywhere and everywhere— and that's a nice place to be.

Bruce, on creativity, interview with Jon Pareles, *New York Times*, September 27, 2017.

Bruce has sold more than 150 million records worldwide, listing him among the best-selling music artists in history.

Born in the U.S.A, released in 1984, remains his best-selling album, selling more than 30 million copies!

CHAPTER
FOUR

NO SURRENDER

For fifty years, Bruce Springsteen
has survived at the top without ever
surrendering his art or identity.
His musical legacy will outlive us all,
a shining light for future generations of
songwriters to follow.

But have you ever wondered how
he stayed so freakin' cool, so relevant,
so fighting fit, for so long?

You're about to find out...

> **"**
>
> As Stevie Van Zandt says:
> Rock 'n' roll…it's a
> band thing.
>
> **"**

Bruce, on rock and roll, Induction into the
Rock 'n Roll Hall of Fame speech, 1999.

66

Love the E Street Band. Can't wait to get onstage with them. Come 2025, it'll be 50 years together. Those are my guys, the greatest band I've ever played with. We do something that's totally unique.

99

Bruce, on the E Street Band, interview with Andy Greene, *Rolling Stone*, November 18, 2022.

> 66
>
> Los Angeles provides a lot of anonymity. You're not like the big fish in the small pond. People wave to you and say 'hi', but you're pretty much left to go your own way. Me in New Jersey, on the other hand, was like Santa Claus at the North Pole.
>
> 99

Bruce, on his near-mythical status, interview with James Henke, *Rolling Stone*, August 6, 1992.

Fame is like you're a bit of a figment of a lot of other people's imaginations. And that always takes some sorting out. But it's even worse when you see yourself as a figment of your own imagination.

Bruce, on fame, interview with James Henke, *Rolling Stone*, August 6, 1992.

Being successful in one area is illusory. People think because you're so good at one particular thing, you're good at many things. And that's almost always not the case. You're good at that particular thing, and the danger is that that particular thing allows you the indulgence to remove yourself from the rest of your life.

Bruce, on being good at only one thing, interview with James Henke, *Rolling Stone*, August 6, 1992.

Bruce has performed live
in front of an audience
approximately 3,500 times.

On average, that's a gig
every five days for 50 years!

I never tell the band, 'We're going to play four hours tonight.' They'd look at me like, 'Oh my God.'

Bruce, on the often three-hour minimum to concert lengths, interview with Andy Greene, *Rolling Stone*, November 18, 2022.

"

I'll tell ya the truth. I really don't want to talk about it. I really don't want to touch on the songs at all because I'll screw them up. As soon as you start talking about it, you're messing with the magic, you know?

"

Bruce, on keeping his song meanings a secret, interview with Jeff Burger, *Zoo World*, March 14, 1974.

I come from a boardwalk town where almost everything is tinged with a bit of fraud. So am I.

Bruce, on Freehold, New Jersey (and himself), interview with Terry Gross, *NPR*, October 5, 2016.

66

By twenty, I was a guitar player on the streets of Asbury Park. But I held four clean aces. I had youth, almost a decade of hard-core bar band experience, a good group of homegrown musicians who were attuned to my performance style and a story to tell.

99

Bruce, on his formative years in New Jersey, interview with Terry Gross, *NPR*, October 5, 2016.

"

I always want my shows to be a little bit like a circus with a touch of political rally. I want people to go away feeling more connected to each other and connected in their own lives and to the whole world around them.

"

Bruce, on concerts as connections, interview with David Hepworth, *Q Magazine*, August 1992.

What was done to our country
was wrong and unpatriotic and
un-American and nobody has
been held to account. There is
a real patriotism underneath
the best of my music, but it
is a critical, questioning and
often angry patriotism.

Bruce, on the Bush/Gore election of 2000 and his political
leanings, interview with Fiachra Gibbons, *The Guardian*,
February 17, 2012.

"

Pessimism and optimism are slammed up against each other in my records, the tension between them is where it's all at, it's what lights the fire.

"

Bruce, on his album's core messaging, interview with Fiachra Gibbons, *The Guardian*, February 17, 2012.

In 2021, Bruce sold
the master recordings
and publishing rights for
his entire music
catalogue to Sony for a
then record-breaking fee
of $500 million dollars.

Yes,
half a billion dollars.

66

All I can do is put my music out there. Of course, I'm interested in having a young audience. I'm interested in whoever's interested in what I'm doing. But all I have to say is, 'This is how I've grown up. These are the places I've been, and these are the things I've learned. Maybe this will have some value.'

99

Bruce, on being honest in his songs, interview with James Henke, *Rolling Stone*, August 6, 1992.

I think an audience always wants two things. They want to feel at home, and they want to be surprised. And I go out every time to do those two things.

Bruce, on giving his fans what they want, interview with Jon Pareles, *New York Times*, September 27, 2017.

"

I didn't grow up in a very political household. The only politics I heard was from my mother. I came home from grade school, where someone asked me if I was Republican or Democrat, and I asked my mom. She said, 'We're Democrats, 'cause Democrats are for the working people.'

"

Bruce, on politics, interview with Jann Wenner, *Rolling Stone*, September 22, 2004.

The bonus I got out of writing 'Streets of Philadelphia' was that all of a sudden a gay man wouldn't be afraid to talk to me. My image had always been very heterosexual, very straight. So it was a nice experience for me, a chance to clarify my own feelings about gay and lesbian civil rights.

Bruce, on 'Streets of Philadelphia', interview with Judy Wieder, *The Advocate*, 1996.

> ❝
>
> One, I would tell him to approach his job like on one hand, it's the most serious thing in the world and on two, as it's only rock and roll. You have to keep both of those things in your head at the same time, simultaneously.
>
> ❞

Bruce, when asked "What advice would old Bruce give his younger self?", interview with Neil Strauss, *Guitar World*, October 1995.

Louder guitars.

Bruce, when asked "What advice would young
Bruce give his older self?", interview with Neil Strauss,
Guitar World, October 1995.

I had success locally and I liked that. I got the attention from the girls. I made a few bucks, not much but I didn't need much. Most importantly, I beat the 9-to-5 thing which I was very interested in doing. I had no practical skills, and I wasn't book-smart at school, so I'd managed to learn this craft that was keeping me afloat.

Bruce, on becoming a local professional musician, interview with Adam Sweeting, *Uncut Magazine*, September 2002.

I was real good at music and real bad at everything else.

Bruce, on life outside of music, interview with James Henke, *Rolling Stone*, August 6, 1992.

66

I never fit in. In the '70s, the music I wrote was sort of romantic, and there was lots of innocence in it, and it certainly didn't feel like it was a part of that particular time. And in the '80s, I was writing and singing about what I felt was happening to the people I was seeing around me or what direction I saw the country going in. And that really wasn't in step with the times, either.

99

Bruce, on fitting in, interview with James Henke, *Rolling Stone*, August 6, 1992.

Music became a hectic obsession, it gave me enormous focus and energy and fire to burn, because it was coming out of pure fear and self-loathing and self-hatred. I'd get onstage and it was hard for me to stop. That's why my shows were so long. They weren't long because I had an idea or a plan that they should be that long. I couldn't stop until I felt burnt, period. Thoroughly burnt.

Bruce, on music as obsession, interview with James Henke, *Rolling Stone*, August 6, 1992.

Music might have been positive for other people, but there was an element of it that was abusive for me. Basically, it was my drug.

Bruce, on music as obsession, interview with James Henke, *Rolling Stone*, August 6, 1992.

I'd played with most of those fellows almost exclusively since I was 18 and I think I reached 40 and I said 'Well, there's a lot of other musicians out there. I want to expose both myself and my music to other influences.'

Bruce, on taking a break from the E Street Band, radio interview with Dutch Radio, May 1993.

"

I always used to say,
'Gee, I'd do it for free, but
don't tell anybody.'

"

Bruce, on playing live, radio interview with RAI,
May 1993.

The best thing I did was I got into therapy. I crashed into myself and saw a lot of myself as I really was. And I questioned all my motivations. Why am I writing what I'm writing? Why am I saying what I'm saying? Do I mean it? Am I bullshitting? Am I just trying to be the most popular guy in town? Do I need to be liked that much? I questioned everything I'd ever done, and it was good. You should do that.

Bruce, on therapy, interview with James Henke, *Rolling Stone*, August 6, 1992.

In 1993, Bruce won the Best Original Song Academy Award for 'Streets of Philadelphia' from Jonathan Demme's film *Philadelphia*. By winning, Bruce became the first rock 'n' roll artist to win an Oscar!

During his acceptance speech, Bruce joked: "This is the first song I ever wrote for a motion picture, so I guess it's all downhill from here.

Money comes in—great! We can let the good times roll; we can have fun with it. But if you start to get caught up in the idea that these things are going to sustain you in some fashion when you get 20 years down the road, you're gonna be in for a surprise.

Bruce, on fame and fortune, interview with Gavin Martin, *NME*, March 9, 1996.

I always felt that the musician's job, as I experienced it growing up, was to provide an alternative source of information, a spiritual and social rallying place, somewhere you went to have a communal experience.

Bruce, on the role of the musician, interview with Jann Wenner, *Rolling Stone*, September 22, 2004.

The past is never the past. It is always present. And you better reckon with it in your life and in your daily experience, or it will get you. It will come and it will devour you, it will remove you from the present. It will steal your future.

Bruce, on the past, interview with Mark Hagen, *The Guardian*, January 18, 2009.

For me, once I count the band in, and I delve deep into my song, I feel a certain sort of integrity and integration that I rarely find in my daily life.

Bruce, on the power of performing live, interview with Jeffrey Brown, *PBS*, December 20, 2016.

I wasn't interested in immediate success or how much each particular record was selling. I was interested in becoming part of peoples' lives and part of fans' lives and hopefully growing up with them together.

Bruce, on establishing a long-term connection with his audience, interview with Neil Strauss, *Guitar World*, October 1995.

CHAPTER
FIVE

TOUGHER THAN THE REST

Bruce has endured 10 U.S. presidents
(many of which he protested vocally)
and way too many disappointing political
decisions that he felt held his country
back from being a land of the free,
and home of the brave.

As America's greatest living lyricist,
Bruce used his words to give a voice to
those that can't speak for themselves.

Why?
Because he's tougher than the rest of us,
as these words of wisdom show...

I don't think about it. I can't get involved in that. Because I learned, don't ever expect anything. I got my hopes, you know, but my hopes are completely based in reality, in what I know I can do.

Bruce, on perhaps one day making it big, interview with Jeff Burger, *Zoo World*, March 14, 1974.

Guys in the group gotta pay alimony, rent, food bills. And a guy may just want to go out for the evening to relax, go to a bar or something and buy a drink, you know?

Bruce, on being the boss (and making sure the band get paid), interview with Jeff Burger, *Zoo World*, March 14, 1974.

This is it for me. I got no choice.
I have to write and play. If I
became an electrician tomorrow,
I'd still come home at night and
write songs. If you can choose,
you might as well quit. But if
you have to, you have to.

Bruce, on music as his only option, interview with
Jeff Burger, *Zoo World*, March 14, 1974.

"

My mother was decent, compassionate, strong, wilful. The best part of me picked up a lot of those characteristics and I struggle to live up to them today. So I think dependability, strength, wilfulness...put in the service of something good—those are the things that matter to me.

"

Bruce, on the qualities he and his mother share, interview with Michael Hann, *The Guardian*, October 30, 2016.

Bruce Springsteen and the E Street Band made their now-legendary live debut on September 20, 1974 at the Tower Theater in Upper Darby, Pennsylvania.

It was the first gig Bruce earned $5,000 for a night's work—more money than he had ever earned up to that point for performing music.

I've always felt that essentially I'm a playing musician. I go out on the road and play; we do live rock 'n' roll shows and everybody has a good time. And then on the side, after that, I write the songs and make albums, but I feel most like myself when I'm playing, when we're doing shows.

Bruce, on where he feels most at home, interview with Dave DiMartino, *Creem Magazine*, January 1981.

I do my best to bring out the best in you, which brings out the best in me.

Bruce, on his live performances, interview with David Hepworth, *Q Magazine*, August 1992.

You have to understand
the limitations of your own
life and keep pushing
through it.

Bruce, on reinvention and pushing boundaries, interview
with David Hepworth, *Q Magazine*, August 1992.

Any time you make your living as a musician, you're way ahead of the game. I always thought: 'Gee, I'm making a living scratching on a piece of wood. I can't complain too much.'

Bruce, on being a professional musician, interview with Michael Hann, *The Guardian*, October 30, 2016.

Home never had a big attraction for me. I get excited staying in all these different hotels, in a whole lot of rooms. I'm always curious what the wallpaper's gonna be like. Do I have a big bed or a little one? And what's this funny painting?

Bruce, on touring as escape, interview with Robert Duncan, *Creem Magazine*, October 1978.

I was very interested in being connected to my home, my home state, my home base. I thought all of these things were very much mine, there wasn't anyone else writing in this way about these things at that time. So it was something I did very intentionally in a sense, as creating a certain very, very specific and original identity.

Bruce, on New Jersey as inspiration and identity, interview with Terry Gross, *NPR*, October 5, 2016.

Musicians, by our nature, we're transient. We move on. There's folks that stay and there's folks that go, and we're folks that go.

Bruce, on his transient lifestyle, interview with Terry Gross, *NPR*, October 5, 2016.

66

You can change someone's life in three minutes with the right song. I still believe that to this day. You can bend the course of their development, what they think is important, of how vital and alive they feel.

99

Bruce, on the power of music, interview with Michael Hann, *The Guardian*, October 30, 2016.

Once the kids came along, I realized I could squeeze my previous 18 hours of workday into six or eight, without any problems whatsoever. I realized the song is always going to be there—there's always going to be a song in your heart or in your head—but kids, they're there and then they're gone. And when they're gone, they're gone. Once I realized that, I found a tremendous freedom from the tyranny of my own mind.

Bruce, on balancing work and home life, interview with Michael Hann, *The Guardian*, October 30, 2016.

The key to the relationship between a band and its audience is that you have to be able to walk out on stage and see yourself in the faces of the crowd. And they gotta be able to see some part of them in you. That's what rock 'n' roll music is all about.

Bruce, on connecting with audiences, radio interview with RAI, May 1993.

The world has become such a brutal place. I think that people go to live music to get in touch with their own humanness and their own humanity. I always thought that's why people came to my shows, and that's why I go on stage and play. It's a life raft to cling to in the world out there.

Bruce, on the importance of live music, radio interview with RAI, May 1993.

I've made the records that I've wanted to make. I think that in the course of probably the BITUSA record, the story I was living overshadowed the story I was telling, and that is the consequence of a certain amount of maybe success and fame.

Bruce, on fame interrupting his narrative, interview with Bob Costas, "Columbia Records Radio Hour", November 21, 1995.

The best music is generally the stuff that you don't know how you did it.

Bruce, on songwriting, interview with Mans Ivarsson, *Beats Magazine*, August 1992

I've got my own oldies now.

Bruce, on his career longevity and performing covers of earlier artists, interview with David Hepworth, *Q Magazine*, August 1992.

"

I lived in New Jersey for a very long time, and I'd written about a lot of things which were very tied into my past, a lot of ghosts you're chasing. In my own life, I was just interested in putting some distance between me and—not New Jersey the state—but whatever some part of that meant for me inside.

"

Bruce, on escaping his past, interview with David Hepworth, Q *Magazine*, August 1992.

I'm 31 and I've been playing in bars since I was 15, and I've faced a lot of audiences that don't give a shit that you're onstage.

Bruce, on performing live and audiences, interview with Dave Dimartino, *Creem Magazine*, January, 1981.

The iconic saxophonist in the E Street Band, Clarence "Big Man" Clemons, was Bruce's musical brother. He died in 2011.

Clarence precisely remembers the night they met: "A rainy, windy night it was, and when I opened the door the whole thing flew off its hinges and blew away down the street. The band were onstage but staring at me framed in the doorway. Bruce and I looked at each other and didn't say anything, we just knew. We knew we were the missing links in each other's lives. He was what I'd been searching for."

When we first started playing, I'd go to every show expecting nobody to come, and I'd go onstage expecting nobody to give me anything for free. And that's the way you have to play. If you don't play like that, pack your guitar up, throw it in the trash can, go home, fix televisions, do some other line of work, you know? Do something where that's the way you feel about it.

Bruce, on giving a performance 100 per cent onstage, interview with Dave DiMartino, *Creem Magazine*, January 1981.

"

I know that my life was changed in an instant by something that people thought was purely junk— pop music records.

"

Bruce, on pop music, interview with Michael Hann, *The Guardian*, October 30, 2016.

> **"**
> I hadn't paid a penny in taxes when I was on the cover of *Time* and *Newsweek*, and the IRS found out about it, and it took me 10 years to pay it.
> **"**

Bruce, on paying his taxes, interview with Jann Wenner, *Rolling Stone*, September 15, 2022.

66

I looked at myself and I just said, 'Well, you know, I can sing but I'm not the greatest singer in the world. I can play guitar very well but I'm not the greatest guitar player in the world.' So I said, 'Well, if I'm going to project an individuality, it's going to have to be in my writing.'

99

Bruce, on deciding to become a songwriter, interview with James R. Petersen, *Playboy*, March 1976.

I think that the E Street Band was a symbolic bridge between me and my audience. When you lead a musician's transient life, the community that you imagined and wrote about, you don't really become a part of. The band was sort of the physical manifestation of those things, your neighbors, and your friends, and the people you've got to live with.

Bruce, on the E Street Band, interview with Neil Strauss, *Guitar World*, October 1995.

There's an intimacy that occurs after hundreds and hundreds and hundreds of nights on stage that is very unique. I'm not sure what I would compare it to. Imagine finding a group of people when you were just out of high school that you did something together with that lasted for 35 years. It's an amazing thing. And it's a gift that life doesn't often afford.

Bruce, on the E Street Band, interview with Neil Strauss, *Guitar World*, October 1995.

When you're nineteen and you're in a truck and you're crossing the country back and forth, and then you're twenty-five and you're on tour with the band—that just fit my personality completely. That's why I was able to be good at it. But then I reached an age where I began to miss my real life—or to even know that there was another life to be lived.

Bruce, on life outside of music, interview with James Henke, *Rolling Stone*, August 6, 1992.

Around the time of *Born in the U.S.A.*, I bought this big house in New Jersey, which was really quite a thing for me to do. It was a place I used to run by all the time. It was a big house, and I said, 'Hey, this is a rich man's house.' And I think the toughest thing was that it was in a town where I'd been spit on when I was a kid.

Bruce, on his hometown, interview with James Henke, *Rolling Stone*, August 6, 1992.

❝

My characters have always been on the move going someplace, searching for something—whether it's a better life or running from something with the idea that somehow moving will make you better, it'll heal you inside. Maybe it's some of my own experience and some of just that's the American story.

❞

Bruce, on running as a leitmotif lyrical theme, interview with Bob Costas, "Columbia Records Radio Hour", November 21, 1995.

I want my records to be heard. At the same time, I want them to be understood.

Bruce, on his music being misunderstood, interview with Bob Costas, "Columbia Records Radio Hour", November 21, 1995.

We throw a big party to make you laugh and dance and the band would act crazy onstage, but behind it was the idea also that you're providing an essential service of some sort. That unspoken promises are made between an audience and an artist, whether you say them or not, they're a part of the dialogue that comes with the turf.

Bruce, on providing a service with each live performance, interview with Adam Sweeting, *Uncut Magazine*, September 2002.

You can't get into a game of ultimately attempting to satisfy your entire audience. It's a losing game. You've just got to play it as it lays and move on. That's the only chance I think you have of remaining vital and alive and grounded.

Bruce, on his audience, interview with Neil Strauss, *Guitar World*, October 1995.

"

I don't gauge the show by the audience reaction; I don't gauge the show by the review in the paper the next day. I know what I did when I'm done. I know if I feel good and I know if I feel bad. I know if I can go to sleep easy that night. That's the way that we judge it and that's the way that we run it.

"

Bruce, on great performances, interview with Dave DiMartino, *Creem Magazine*, January 1981.

Politics and life go hand in hand. And so it needed to be a part of my music. The different social forces that affected my parents' lives or my friends' lives or I saw around me became essential for me to write about.

Bruce, on politics in music, interview with Jeffrey Brown, *PBS*, December 20, 2016.

C H A P T E R
SIX

THE BOSS

Bruce may dislike his famous term of
endearment—The Boss—because
as the Man sang himself, "I ain't here on
business, baby, I'm only here for fun."
But, whether he liked it or not, Bruce has
always been leading the charge.

Last, but by no means least, let's
dive deep into the Boss's best
soundbites; the words, the wit, the
wisdom, and the wry wisecrackin'
that defined a 50-year career in
showbusiness that never knew when
to quit. Thank God.

People thought 'Born to Run' had been a record company creation. We had to reprove our viability on a nightly basis, by playing, and it took many years.

Bruce, on his early fame and success, interview with Keith Cameron, *The Guardian*, September 23, 2010.

I tend to be not my own best company. So I can get a little lost if I don't have my work to occasionally focus me.

Bruce, on his depression and work ethic, interview with Terry Gross, *NPR*, October 5, 2016.

66

I hate being called 'Boss'.
Always did from the beginning.
I hate bosses. I hate being
called the boss. It just started
from all the people around
me, then by somebody on the
radio and once that happens,
everybody said, 'Hey, Boss,' and
I'd say, 'No. Bruce. *BRUCE.*'

99

Bruce, on being the Boss, interview with Dave DiMartino,
Creem Magazine, January 1981.

66

Everybody sings their own spirit, their own personality, it's like a fingerprint; no two musicians play the same or bring to the stage something similar.

99

Bruce, on being different to other artists, interview with David Hepworth, *Q Magazine*, August 1992.

I always wanted my shows to be fun where you could come and dance. I wanted my records to be the kind you could vacuum the floor to if you wanted to or help you make some kind of sense of the world you live in. There's nothing particularly that I couldn't see myself writing about.

Bruce, on subjects for songwriting, interview with David Hepworth, *Q Magazine*, August 1992.

"

I tend to like to play inside. Even in a big place. I just feel it's appropriate for my music. I don't know why. There should be smoke and sweat.

"

Bruce, on his venue preferences, interview with David Hepworth, *Q Magazine*, August 1992.

"America's future rests in a thousand dreams inside our hearts. It rests in the message of hope in the songs of a man so many young Americans admire: New Jersey's own Bruce Springsteen," so said then-President Ronald Reagan in a 1984 election campaign speech in Hammonton, New Jersey referencing Bruce's "nationalistic" song "Born in the U.S.A."

Sadly, Reagan and many others misinterpreted the message of "Born in the U.S.A."—a song that confronted the emptiness of the American Dream, not celebrated it.

66

People think it was rock that brought me to the music scene. But that's all wrong. What got me playing, in fact, was soul, and the way soul bands used to operate. Mainly the way they can create an almost spiritual experience.

99

Bruce, on soul music, interview with Mans Ivarsson, *Beats Magazine*, August 1992.

When the *Tunnel of Love* tour ended in 1989, I needed to do something new, but I didn't have the nerve. I went through a very confusing time, a depression, really. I began to reassess everything I'd gone through. Like the success I'd had with *Born in the U.S.A.* Did I like it? Did I want to do something like that again? Was I misunderstood? I also thought a lot about the iconic status that my music had attained. Sure, my music had always had a mythic edge to it, but I just felt overwhelmed by everything. I felt dehumanized.

Bruce, on his mental health in the late 1980s, interview with Mans Ivarsson, *Beats Magazine*, August 1992.

"

When I was young, I truly didn't think music had any limitations. I thought it could give you everything you wanted in life.

"

Bruce, on the power of music, interview with David Sinclair, *Rolling Stone*, June 24, 1993.

"

All I try to do is to write
music that feels meaningful
to me, that has commitment
and passion behind it. And
I guess I feel that if what
I'm writing about is real,
and if there's emotion, then
hey, there'll be somebody
who wants to hear it.

"

Bruce, on writing real from the heart, interview with
James Henke, *Rolling Stone*, August 6, 1992.

When I separated from the E Street
Band, there was tremendous
feedback from the fans. Some fans
were hurt because I think one of
the values of my music was about
loyalty, friendship, and remembering
the past. So, at some point, the
question becomes how do you stay
true to those values but yet grow
up and become your own man?

Bruce, on pleasing his fans, interview with Neil Strauss,
Guitar World, October 1995.

"

I'm telling a story and I'm really only in the middle of it.

"

Bruce, on his career, interview with James Henke, *Rolling Stone*, August 6, 1992.

"

In the end, the only thing
you can do is destroy
what you create. So when
I wrote *Tunnel of Love*, I
thought I had to reintroduce
myself as a songwriter,
in a very non-iconic role.
And it was a relief.

"

Bruce, on reinventing his sound, interview with
James Henke, *Rolling Stone*, August 6, 1992.

66

Music came along, and I latched onto it as a way to combat the isolationist part of myself. Music was a way that I could talk to people. It provided me with a means of communication, a means of placing myself in a social context—which I had a tendency not to want to do.

99

Bruce, on music as a social connection, interview with James Henke, *Rolling Stone*, August 6, 1992.

Hardcore
Springsteen fans are
known as
"Bruce Tramps".

"

The two of the best days of my life were the day I picked up the guitar and the day that I learned how to put it down. Somebody said, 'Man, how did you play for so long?' I said: 'That's the easy part. It's stopping that's hard.'

"

Bruce, on music as obsession, interview with James Henke, *Rolling Stone*, August 6, 1992.

I want to sing about who I am now. I want to get up onstage and sing with all of the 42 years that are in me. When I was young, I always said I didn't want to end up being 45 or 50 and pretending I was 15 or 16 or 20. That just didn't interest me.

Bruce, on staying relevant in the music industry, interview with James Henke, *Rolling Stone*, August 6, 1992.

"

To be sitting here with the kids, Patti, my music— it's a nice seat.

"

Bruce, on domestic and professional bliss, interview with Bill Flanagan, *Musician*, November 1992.

66

I like the smell of the guitars and the amps.

99

Bruce, on being a touring musician, interview with MTV Europe, March 1993.

I don't want to be sitting on my porch when I'm 60 saying, 'Oh, I shoulda, I coulda, I woulda!' You got one ride. So, I said, 'Let's go!'

Bruce, on being the first rock star to grace the cover of *Time* magazine in 1975, interview with Bill Flanagan, *Musician*, November 1992.